An Eagle's Tale

THIS EDITION
Editorial Management by Oriel Square
Produced for DK by WonderLab Group LLC
Jennifer Emmett, Erica Green, Kate Hale, *Founders*

Editor Maya Myers; **Photography Editor** Nicole DiMella; **Managing Editor** Rachel Houghton;
Designers Project Design Company; **Researcher** Michelle Harris;
Copy Editor Lori Merritt; **Indexer** Connie Binder; **Proofreader** Susan K. Hom;
Authenticity Reader Dr. Naomi R. Caldwell; **Series Reading Specialist** Dr. Jennifer Albro

First American Edition, 2024
Published in the United States by DK Publishing, a division of Penguin Random House LLC
1745 Broadway, 20th Floor, New York, NY 10019

Copyright © 2024 Dorling Kindersley Limited
24 25 26 27 10 9 8 7 6 5 4 3 2 1
001-342889-Sep/2024

A catalog record for this book is available from the Library of Congress.
HC ISBN: 978-0-5938-4721-3
PB ISBN: 978-0-5938-4720-6

DK books are available at special discounts when purchased in bulk for sales promotions, premiums, fund-raising,
or educational use. For details, contact:
DK Publishing Special Markets, 1745 Broadway, 20th Floor, New York, NY 10019
SpecialSales@dk.com

Printed and bound in China

The publisher would like to thank the following for their kind permission to reproduce their images:
a=above; c=center; b=below; l=left; r=right; t=top; b/g=background
Alamy Stock Photo: All Canada Photos / Jared Hobbs 12-13, Blickwinkel / Baesemann 18-19,
Design Pics Inc / John Hyde 18b, Pamela Winter 7br; **Dreamstime.com:** Kurt Adams 5br, Tony Bosse 15bc,
Dee Carpenter 9bc, Michele Cornelius 20b, Flying2lowak 21cb, Glebtarro 21br, Brian Kushner 15br, Leshabu 17br,
Maigi 4b, Meunierd 14-15, Ruben Paz 10b, Stefan Schug 14b, Michael Truchon 1, Sergey Uryadnikov 11bc,
23tl, Wirestock 23cla; **Getty Images:** 500px / Brad Balfour 3, Moment / David G Hemmings 4-5,
The Image Bank / Mark Newman 7; **Getty Images / iStock:** BirdImages 22, Dee Carpenter Photography 8bc,
E+ / DaveAlan 17bc, Holcy 12b, Imagexphoto 5bl, Tammi Mild 13b, Moment / Michael J. Cohen, Photographer 8-9,
Pchoui 16-17, 23bl, Predrag1 6b, Supercaliphotolistic 16b, USO 10-11, 20-21; **KHNS:** Henry Leasia 19crb, 23cl;
Native Stock Pictures: Marilyn Angel Wynn 19bl; **Shutterstock.com:** AnW Studios LLC 9br, Kavram 5bc;
USFWS: Dave Menke 7bc, NCTC Image Library / Lisa Hupp 11br

Cover images: *Front:* **Dreamstime.com:** Taras Adamovych (Eagle);
Getty Images / iStock: Oleksandra Klestova (Background); *Back:* **Dreamstime.com:** Olga Puseva cra

All other images © Dorling Kindersley Limited
For more information see: www.dkimages.com

www.dk.com

MIX
Paper | Supporting
responsible forestry
FSC™ C018179

This book was made with Forest
Stewardship Council™ certified
paper – one small step in DK's
commitment to a sustainable future.
Learn more at
www.dk.com/uk/information/sustainability

An Eagle's Tale

Angela Modany

DK

tree

An eagle flies in the sky.
It is spring.
The eagle looks
for a tree.
It builds a nest
in the tree.

The eagle lays
eggs in the nest.
The eagle sits
on the eggs.
This keeps the
eggs warm.
The eggs hatch!
The baby eagles are
called chicks.

egg

rabbit

The chicks are hungry.
The eagle leaves to
hunt for food.
It hunts for fish, rabbits,
and squirrels.

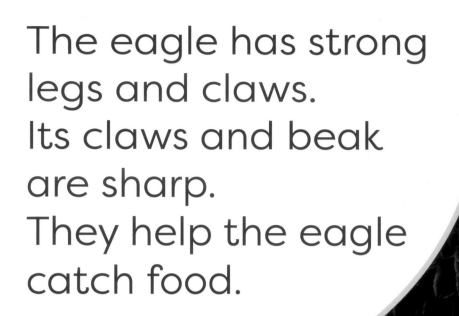

The eagle has strong
legs and claws.
Its claws and beak
are sharp.
They help the eagle
catch food.

beak

The chicks eat.
The chicks grow bigger.
They learn to fly.
Then, the chicks leave
the nest.

nest

feather

People watch the eagle
in the summer.
The eagle drops its
old feathers.
This gives room for new
feathers to grow.
The people gather
the feathers.
The feathers are
special to the people.

It is fall.
The eagle flies far.
It flies to a river.
There are salmon
in the river.
The eagle
eats salmon.

salmon

festival

Many eagles come to
eat the salmon.
The people honor
the eagles.
They have a festival.
The people tell stories
about the eagles.

river

It is winter.
It is very cold.
The eagle leaves
the river.
The eagle flies far.

The eagle goes back
to its nest.
In spring, it will lay
more eggs.
There will be eagle
chicks again!

Glossary

claw
the sharp nail on an animal's toe

fly
to travel through the air

gather
to bring together

honor
to treat something with respect

strong
having great power

Quiz

Answer the questions to see what you have learned. Check your answers with an adult.

1. Where do eagles build their nests?

2. What are baby eagles called?

3. What are some things eagles eat?

4. What do eagles drop?

5. What do the eagles eat from the river?

1. In trees 2. Chicks 3. Fish, rabbits, and squirrels 4. Feathers
5. Salmon